The Employer's Handbook for Public Safety Negotiations

Negotiating Without Confrontation and Crisis

Ronald J. York
President of POLICEPAY.NET, Inc.

POLICEPAY.NET, Inc.
219 West Boyd Street; Suite 205
Norman, Oklahoma 73069

Telephone: (405) 701-8616
Facsimile: (405) 701-8631

E-mail: editor@policepay.net

http://www.policepay.net

The Employer's Handbook for Public Safety Negotiations by
Ronald J. York
Cover design, editing, and typesetting by Charles L. Wonsey

A POLICEPAY.NET, Inc. Publication

Published by POLICEPAY.NET, Inc.
Printed in the United States of America
First Edition
ISBN: 978-0-6151-6394-9

Acknowledgements

My thanks go out to Charles Wonsey for his work editing my manuscript and formatting it to create this book. I am also thankful for the hundreds of clients that have hired me to negotiate their contracts. Without the knowledge I've gained throughout my years of experience, this book would never have been possible. And finally, I thank you, my new reader, for getting past the fact that I have often worked as the "competition" at public safety negotiations and for understanding that my goal is to simplify the negotiations process for all those involved. I promise, this book isn't just a trick to get you to make mistakes at the table to make my job easier. If you are still worried, go ahead and hire me to negotiate for your side and you'll see that I follow my own instruction as well.

Preface

Many times I suspect that people view me as a bellowing loud mouth. I know what they are thinking. Okay Mr. Wisenheimer, how did you get to be so smart about contract negotiations? I even ask myself that question on occasion. Negotiating is like walking into a giant labyrinth that has many dead ends. I have discovered some of those dead ends. This handbook is designed to steer you away from them. While I may not lead you to the exit, I should greatly increase your chances of finding it on your own.

I could take any hole, on any golf course, and tell you exactly which clubs to use and how to play them to obtain par. First, you tee off with a Number 1 driver, keeping the ball to the left. Next, you use the 5 iron to put the ball on the front part of the green. This is followed by using the putter to get the ball close to the pin. And finally, you use the putter to tap the ball in for par. Are you listening Tiger? I guarantee this result, provided that everything cooperates – your body, the grass, the wind, the humidity, the fairway, the green, etc. Unfortunately, everything does not always cooperate.

Sometimes the ball goes into the rough or the sand trap. I have seen a ball defy gravity and refuse to drop into the cup. Even Tiger occasionally experiences these phenomenas.

My experience in public safety contract negotiations goes back nearly forty years and I am still finding new dead ends. I wish that I could tell you that I have things down to an exact science. I can show you how to never lose at tic-tac-toe, but negotiating is not that simple. I have spent most of my time negotiating for employees and observing employer negotiators. I used to get so frustrated with employers. Why can they not see how stupid their tactics are and just do things correctly? Oh, I was ready to do a complete makeover on the people on the other side of the table. After holding those thoughts for some time, actually many years, I began to realize that I, as well as the people I represented, were really doing the same thing as the employer. Realizing that what I had been doing was actually counterproductive, I decided to apply the wisdom of the serenity prayer. I embarked on a mission to change the things I had the power to change – myself. This led to a totally different way of negotiating. Soon, I wanted to convert the whole world to my way of negotiating. Actually, I had not discovered anything new, but only existing knowledge that was not being frequently used. Suddenly, I ran into a new road block. I might be able to change myself, but I could not really change another person. They have to want to change and to do it themselves.

About twenty years ago, I began writing articles and presenting seminars for policemen and firefighters that taught my negotiating methods. A lot of people have read my articles and attended my seminars. Some have completely embraced my teachings. Others, including friends, have actually disagreed with what I teach. They just find it hard to let go of the habits of the past. I am not the only voice on the stage. There are others, mostly attorneys, advocating confrontation and hostilities. To people such as police officers, who work in that type of environment daily, fighting has a certain appeal. It is sometimes hard to separate the street from other aspects of life.

The purpose of writing this book is to help if you want to change how you negotiate with your employees. But, just as it is with them, I cannot make you change. You have to do it. You ask, why would I want to change? I would answer you by saying that it is in your best interest. If, after reading this book, you do not feel that utilizing the concepts presented is in your best interest, then do not adopt them. But remember, your best interest must be considered in a universal context. Simply looking at a narrow and current interest is not enough. Stealing a candy bar to obtain present gratification may be in your best interest at moment, but if you have to go to jail as the result, it is probably not in your best interest globally. Negotiations are no different. Beating down your opponent at the negotiating table to obtain the lowest price may get other results that you do not anticipate – retaliation by your employees. Agreeing to an amount that is higher than what it should be to pacify your employees can be just as imprudent.

This is what I ask of you. If you find something that I say that does not square with rationale, ignore it. Keep in mind that dogma is not rationale. When we discuss the impact of step pay plans, I really hope that you will use your brain and get rid of your dogma. This is the one area where I have seen truly intelligent people behave like doped up zealots. I hope you will not be one of those. There is nothing wrong with being totally committed to your side and its goals, but at least be honest with yourself.

Table of Contents

Introduction

This book is the companion to my earlier book – The Police Negotiator's Handbook. That book was written from the perspective of a person negotiating on behalf of the employees. This book is written from the perspective of the employer. The first chapter of this book, Research Evidence, is almost a verbatim duplicate of the first chapter of my previous book. Each side needs the same set of facts. However, everything after Chapter One is different. Think of it like football. Both the offensive and defensive teams have eleven players and both line up in similar and complementary formation, but that is where the similarities end. In collective bargaining, the employees are the offensive team and the employer is on defense. One important distinction between football and negotiating is that there is no score keeping in negotiations. If you see your goal as out-scoring your counterparts, you are probably dooming any chance of success in negotiations. Negotiating is the only competition where the goal is to play to a tie – a deal that leaves both sides feeling that the outcome is fair and equal for those involved.

You may think that I am trying to give insider information to the unions through my previous book, and I am now giving opposing and contradictory instructions to city negotiators. I am not. Each side has a different role. Knowing and understanding the other side's perspective increases the chances of a reasonable agreement being obtained. Keep in mind that reasonable means reasonable for both sides, not just your side. Contract negotiations do not have to be a war with a winner and a loser. You certainly do not want it be a love fest, but it can be cooperative and collaborative. Think about a transaction between a business and a customer. Does the customer really want a purchase price that is so low that the business goes broke? It is rather hard to collect on a guarantee from a business that no longer exists. Does the business really want a profit so large that the customer never comes back for more business or service? Many businesses depend on after-sale services to be a financial success. Most people want a price that is perceived as fair to both parties and that will sustain the relationship. One thing that really amuses me, is how most paid negotiators are compensated – by the time worked, not the results. For many attorney negotiators there is no monetary incentive to obtain a deal within a reasonable length of time. Actually, a protracted and highly adversarial negotiating process not only yields large fees, it creates future contract grievance business as the result of the acrimony generated by the hostile environment. Your objective should be to get to the proper deal without damaging the product and the relationship in the process.

I have written this book as if the union is doing all of the wrong things during negotiations and they probably will be. In the unlikely event that they are doing things correctly, the process should be much easier for you and them. In the book for union negotiators, I assumed that the city would be doing all of the wrong things, which is also correct most of the time. Later, we will be discussing what your goal should be and how to go about obtaining it. You need to be 100 percent focused on that goal at all times. Forget about the score and defeating "your opponent." What counts is the result, not the process. A commonly misunderstood adage is "the end does not justify the means." Well, if it doesn't, I do not know what does. What counts is the "end" you end up with. Many people destroy the end with the means they use to seek it. A police officer that chases a speeder through town at 100 miles per hour and kills two people and wrecks ten cars, but apprehends the speeder, does not get the end he sought – to make his town safe from speeders. A city negotiator that demoralizes and angers the employees while getting the lowest deal possible is committing the same sin. The value is determined by what you get for what you have to give up.

This handbook is presented in six stages:

- Stage One – Research Evidence
- Stage Two – Develop Relationships
- Stage Three – Establish Your Authority
- Stage Four – Develop Trust with Union
- Stage Five – Negotiate the Deal
- Stage Six – Get the Deal Ratified

Obviously, the ideal application of these stages is sequential. Each stage leads into the next. Unfortunately, I cannot write this book like a cookbook that will give perfect results by just strictly adhering to the recipe. You will have to be able to "think on your feet" and make on-site adjustments. I could teach you the technique of the double play, but it would do you no good if there is no double play situation, or if the first runner has too big of a lead, or if the pitcher failed to cover first base. There are all kinds of possibilities. You have to remain flexible.

The first chapter will tell you what research you need to do. Use that research to develop your thoughts and positions. To be able to reason with a person, that person's positions must be the result of reasoning. That applies to you, not just the people you have to deal with. If your positions are not based on reason, get rid of them.

CHAPTER 1

Stage One:

Research Evidence

Whether you are the employer or the union, it all begins with research. Without the facts and the knowledge provided by research, you have no way of knowing what the proper outcome of negotiations should be. There are seven steps to research. All seven are very important. What kind of research should you do? I am going to list the reports that must be generated and what they should include. It should then become obvious what data you will need to collect. Each of the seven steps to research result in a report being generated, these steps include:

- The turnover report
- The staffing report
- The recruitment report
- The exit interviews report
- The pay and benefits survey
- The costing analysis

- The ability-to-pay study

Step One – The Turnover Report

A turnover report compares the number of employees leaving the department annually to the total employee count. For example, a department with 300 employees that loses 15 employees during a year has a turnover rate of 5 percent (15 divided by 300 or losses divided by total employees). Data should be collected and reported year-by-year for the last 10 years. To make the report even more valuable, separate the controllable and uncontrollable exits. An employee that separates due to retirement, becoming permanently disabled, or death would be considered an uncontrollable exit. Those who quit or get fired prior to retirement are normally considered controllable exits. A firing is usually a bad hiring decision.

Step Two – The Staffing Report

A staffing report compares the actual number of employees to the authorized strength and the city's population. Data should be collected and reported year-by-year for the last 10 years.

Step Three – The Recruitment Report

The recruitment report measures both the quality and quantity of applicants and recruits. The data should be reported on either a year-by-year basis or by academy classes and should include:

- Total applicants compared to available positions
- Number surviving initial screening
- Number surviving entrance exam
- Number surviving background check
- Number accepted into academy

- Number surviving academy
- Number actually hired
- Number still employed after first year
- Number still employed after second year
- Number still employed after third year
- Number still employed after fourth year
- Number still employed after fifth year

The quality portion should include the following:

- Average education level
- Average entrance test scores
- Average age at time of application

Data should be collected and reported year-by-year for the last 10 years. If your department has not tracked this information historically, now is the time to start.

Step Four - The Exit Interviews Report

This report should show why people left and where they went. Include only those who voluntarily resign prior to retirement. Report the following:

- Number going to other public safety departments
- Number going to a career outside of public safety
- Number leaving for something other than a better job
- Number leaving for better pay
- Number leaving because of management
- Number leaving because they do not like working in public safety

Step Five – The Pay and Benefits Survey

The most reliable pay survey is done on a total compensation basis. The survey must include all forms of compensation that can be reasonably measured. The number of hours that have to be worked each year must be computed for an accurate comparison. To arrive at this number, take the number of hours in a normal work week multiplied by 52 and subtract all available paid time off. Do this year-by-year for years 1 through 30.

When subtracting the paid time off, include the following benefits and deduct them from the normal hours worked:

- Vacation leave
- Holiday leave
- Personal leave
- Sick leave

Now that you have determined the number of hours an employee is required to work during each year, divide the total compensation value by the total hours worked to arrive at the hourly rate for each hour actually spent on the job. The best point of comparison is obtained by averaging all 30 years, thereby comparing only a single number – the hourly rate for a 30-year career.

When calculating the total compensation value, be certain to include the value of the following benefits:

- Base pay
- Longevity
- Shift differentials
- Holiday pay
- Uniform allowance
- Education pay
- Pension contribution pickup

- Employer pension contribution
- Employer health insurance contribution
- Employer retiree insurance contribution
- F.I.C.A. employer contribution

For a valid survey, the agencies included in the survey must be similar departments. Comparability should be based primarily upon size and geographic location. The smaller your department, the closer the comparison sites should be to you geographically. It may make sense for Chicago to compare to New York and Los Angeles because there are not comparably sized cities in their local market. It does not make sense, however, for Peoria to compare with Santa Monica or Yonkers when cities of similar size to Peoria can be located within the same region. Adjustments for the differences in the local cost of living must be made when measuring departments outside of the immediate market. A salary of $50,000 in San Francisco is not the same as a salary of $50,000 in Birmingham. There are several resources for a cost of living index. ACCRA's COLI is the most prevalent.

Once the survey has been compiled, determine where your department should fall in the survey. One agency belongs in first and another should be in last. Not every agency belongs at the average. Typically, larger departments in cities with a higher per capita personal income pay more. This is not always true, but most of the time this relationship is evident.

Step Six – The Costing Analysis

The best way to calculate the cost of a base pay raise is to use the current operating budget. Do not be concerned with what is budgeted for the current year, but rather what was actually spent last year. Many times, the budgeted amount is greatly inflated because there is no allowance for vacancies. The numbers shown in the audited financial statements are more reliable. Unfortunately, there is seldom enough detail to make the necessary computations. In the budget, there is a column for the prior year. It is usually labeled as "Current Year Estimate." This is because the fiscal year has not yet ended when the budget is prepared. The city takes the expenditures to date and estimates additional spending through year end. This is usually the most accurate data available.

Only calculate the cost of a 1 percent base pay raise. Other amounts can be determined by multiplying the 1 percent value. Start by determining the total annual base pay amount for the ranks covered by the union contract. This should be the base number that all other costs are computed from. For these calculations, only items that are affected by a base pay increase should be included. If the average longevity is 15 percent of base pay, then multiply the total base pay cost by 15 percent. If longevity is stated in flat dollar amounts, e.g. 200 dollars per year, do not include it. The most common "roll up" costs are:

- Longevity pay
- Shift pay
- Holiday pay
- FICA contributions by the employer
- Pension contributions by the employer
- Overtime costs

Everything that will increase as the result of a base pay raise should be measured. Do not include step pay raises. Step pay raises do not increase the total payroll. Step pay raises are offset by savings from retirements and terminations.

Step Seven – The Ability-To-Pay Study

What is "ability-to-pay?" If you are trying to buy a house with a mortgage payment of $5,000 per month and your take home pay is $4,000 per month that is an ability to pay problem. Even if your take home pay is $6,000 per month you probably would still have a problem. However, if you have a take home pay of $20,000 per month, but have chosen to own a yacht, a condo in Aspen, three SUVs and a membership in an exclusive country club, all requiring monthly payments that leave you with only $3,000 per month for the mortgage payment, you do not have an ability to pay problem. You simply have to decide what you want. This is called establishing priorities. If the threshold to overcome the ability to pay issue is having enough money to do everything you could possibly ever want and still have $5,000 per month left over, then you might as well move into a pasteboard box under the nearest overpass, because you will never have an extra five gees each month.

The easiest way for the employer to deal with this issue is to not use ability-to-pay as an excuse for not paying the market price for compensation. However, virtually every city will claim that it cannot afford to increase pay. Seldom is this actually true. A typical city has a long-term per capita growth rate for revenues that exceeds the long-term growth rate of wages. On the city's side, ability-to-pay could more accurately be called willingness-to-pay. Most cities have the money. They just have other places that they want to spend their money.

Think of employee compensation like the purchase of street asphalt. You would probably laugh if I suggested that you ask the asphalt plant to sell your city asphalt at a price below the market price because tax revenues are not high enough to pay the going rate. I am certain that the asphalt plant would find that approach amusing. What would be your options if you did not have enough money? You could either buy a smaller quantity of asphalt or a lower quality of asphalt. Every product and service on the face of the earth has three supply and demand variables:

- Quality
- Quantity
- Price

All three elements apply to both the seller (the union) and the buyer (the city). Each entity can control only two of the elements. Based on these two controlled elements, the marketplace determines the third. If the city wants to determine the price and the quantity, it will have to accept the quality of applicants that the marketplace will yield. If the city wants to set the standards for quality and quantity, it will then have to pay the price demanded by the market. If the city is currently getting its desired quality and quantity, its needs are being met and there is no reason to pay more. Most cities believe their needs are being met because they have not fully researched what they are getting for the price they are paying. The answers are found in the first four research reports from Stage One:

- Turnover Report
- Staffing Report
- Recruitment Report
- Exit Interviews Report

Even if recruitment and retention are not currently a problem, they will be if the city does not maintain its competitive position in the market. Today's market leader that does not move above the current status quo soon becomes the last place loser.

If your city is truly strapped for money, which very few are, then the city needs to cut services, not try to get labor, materials, and supplies at submarket prices. Notice I said try. Getting things at something less than the market price is an illusion. Oh, you pay the lower price, but you do not get the product you want. What if you went to Lexus dealership to buy a new car? You want a new Lexus, but you quickly learn that the price is $60,000. Wow, you tell the salesman that you only want to pay $40,000. He says he can do that and immediately shows you a fully load Toyota. You explain to him that you want a Lexus, not a Toyota. He then shows you a two year old used Lexus. By now you are getting frustrated and tell him that you want a brand new Lexus and you only want to pay $40,000. He then explains that you can have a new Lexus or you can pay $40,000, but you cannot do both. On the other hand, it would be foolish to offer $70,000 for the Lexus if it can be obtained for $60,000. Paying something other than market price is not an option. You have to decide what it is you want and what you want to pay. If the price does not yield what you want, you have to reconcile the difference. You can either pay less and get less or pay more and get more. The same principle applies to everything known to man.

Skip the ability to pay argument. It is a lie. The union knows it is a lie. Tell them the truth, whatever it is. The city might be satisfied with the product the current pay scale yields, or maybe it only wants a slight improvement. Maybe the city wants less than what it is currently getting. Whatever the REASONING, base your case on that, not some red herring. The city does not have to increase pay a dime if it does not want to. It is better to discuss the real rationale than to promote some transparent lie. To get what you want or need does not require the selling of snake oil.

CHAPTER 2

Stage Two:

Establish Relationships

To be effective you need to develop a working relationship with the key people within the government. This would include:

1. The administrator (mayor or manager)
2. The chief
3. The finance director
4. The human resources director
5. The city attorney
6. The city council

Your relationship with each of these people needs to be different, because your needs from each is different.

The Administrator

This is the primary and most important relationship. The administrator is the ultimate decision maker. If he is not, then the city has a dysfunctional management team and you might want to reconsider whether you should work for this government. As the city's negotiator you are essentially the alter ego of the administrator. If he is powerless, so are you. The administrator must embrace you being hired as the negotiator. He must trust you and you must trust him. Many things said between you and he will not be shared with others on the list. Later, we will be talking about determining your authority, which will come primarily from the administrator. You will be relying on him for direction and he will be also relying on you for results. If you cannot effectively establish this relationship with the administrator you should resign.

The Chief

The chief needs to be your partner in negotiations as it relates to matters concerning the operation of the department. No one is going to listen to him about pay issues, but on matters such as grievances, discipline, and promotions he will be the ultimate decision maker. The administrator may know how to prepare a budget, but has no idea how to run a police or fire department. That is why he has a chief. It is just like you hiring an electrician. You know nothing about wiring and electricity, and furthermore, you don't want to know. You just want the job done promptly and correctly.

The Three Bureaucrats

The finance director, the human resources director, and the city attorney are typically deal breakers, not deal makers. Forget this at you own peril. If not handled correctly, any or all of them can start shooting out the tires on your bus. Each believes that contract negotiations should revolve around their area of expertise. When that does not occur each tries to inject poison pills to kill any deal made without them. The finance director starts claiming that the city is close to bankruptcy. The human resources director puts out information showing that the current wages and benefits are the best within 500 miles. And lastly, the city attorney starts finding new and creative legal road blocks. To make matters even worse, you will actually need their help. So your goal is not only to get them to drop their weapons, but to actually assist you. This may all sound funny, but getting these folks to behave and cooperate is not always easy. Sure, there are those who do the right thing from the start, but do not count on it.

Maybe you are the human resources director and you have been chosen to be the city's negotiator. Watch out, the finance and legal guys may be more difficult with you than a total stranger. The problem you will have is that the other two have about the same relationship with and access to the administrator. From the administrator's perspective, you are their peer. The time to deal with these people is early on, before they begin an offensive. The administrator may have a global view of the city but the bureaucrats have parochial and turf perspectives.

The City Council

Your goal with the city council is to get them to a level of comfort with you. Let the administrator do most of the talking. One thing you want to be absolutely certain about is the amount of support the administrator has from the council. Any monetary deal will eventually require appropriations that must be approved by the council. You want to be absolutely certain that you and the administrator have sufficient backing from the council. Nothing is more disappointing than having to renegotiate a tentative agreement with the council. Normally, this results in the union voting down the modified agreement. Have the votes counted prior to the start of negotiations.

Part of a good relationship is having a written agreement and not just one that explains what you will be paid and when. The agreement should also be an understanding of your responsibilities and the responsibilities of the various people within the city — all of the people listed above. Management has to be aware of your style and accept it. Obviously, the first step of the relationship is getting hired as the negotiator. The best way of getting appointed is by the administrator, not by the council. The administrator will probably want to get the council's blessing, but try to avoid a formal voir dire by the council. It will weaken the administrator's power and your influence with him. You do not want the council in the decision-making loop. Their influence should be informal and directly with the administrator and should be restricted to helping set the parameters.

By the time you are appointed, you should already have established the proper relationship with the administrator. The first person to deal with after being appointed is the chief, followed by the three bureaucrats. After that, you will want to have a brief meeting with the city council. They need to see you and become comfortable with you. Have an understanding with the administrator about how this meeting will be handled. Let him be in charge. You do not need to dazzle and charm them with your knowledge and experience, just make them comfortable.

CHAPTER 3

Stage Three:

Establish Your Authority

It amazes me how many paid negotiators have no idea what their goal and authority are. If you do not know this you are just an overpaid stenographer, a water boy, a cardboard stand up. If the administrator has not told you what your goal is and has not vested you with enough authority to accomplish that goal, pick up what's left of your self-esteem and get out of Dodge. I am not talking about the city giving you carte blanche authority, but if you simply attend the negotiations sessions as a toothless tiger, taking notes on a legal pad to give to the administrator, it is time to sing that old Johnny Paycheck song – "Take This Job and Shove It." You have to be firm with the people who have employed you. That can be somewhat tricky if you are a full-time city employee. Over the past twenty years, I have spent more time negotiating with my clients than the people on the other side of the negotiating table. I have said "NO" to my clients ten times as many times as I have to my counterparts.

Being an effective negotiator involves risk. You cannot succeed being a wooden dummy like Charlie McCarthy.

You must be absolutely clear about the goals of the negotiations, your authority, and the process of approving any agreements that are obtained. Do not expect the city people to do this. You will have to lead them through it. You will have to do most of the research and determine what the goals are and then have them buy in. Most cities will have either no goal or some nonsense goal such as "let's get them for as little as we can." That type of goal is as realistic as buying a lottery ticket to fund your retirement.

How would that authority be articulated? Try this. The administrator says to you:

> "Based on the research, we believe we are about 3 percent behind the market average. To get the recruitment and retention rates we want, we probably need to be slightly above the market average. Based on our estimates, an annual raise of 4.5 percent for each of the next three years would get us to that point. We might entertain a 7.5 percent increase now and 3 percent each of the next two years, but that may be a tough sale to the council and the public. Anything in excess of 13.5 percent over three years will need to have either an offset from a reduction in some other benefit or possibly a relaxation in some of the work rules. We would prefer to just keep it a clean base pay increase by itself. Based on the rumor mill, the union will be asking for three increases of 6 percent each year, plus some other enhancements. They can forget that. It is not going to happen. We would prefer to dispose of all of the monetary items, other than base pay. If the union is adamant about some of these issues, we may be willing to agree, but they will have to be paid for by a reduction in the base pay raise."

That little statement is about all you need. How far should your authority go? It should allow you to enter into a tentative agreement, provided it falls within the parameters of your instructions. Anything outside those instructions would require approval from the administrator. Getting the council on board is his problem. However, you must be certain that your given authority is within the city's actual expectations. Do not go into negotiations with some ridiculous authority level, such as "you have authority up to 2 percent per year." If that is how it is going to be done, the administrator needs to be doing the negotiating. Do not let him use you as a wimpy stooge. Sometimes you need to give the administrator the same speech Bill Parcells gave Jerry Jones when he accepted the Dallas Cowboys coaching job – "the minute you start trying to run the team, I'm out of here."

In addition, you will need to have an understanding with the administrator that he will force the chief and the three bureaucrats to correctly participate in the process. This is especially important concerning the chief. When you start dealing with non-monetary operational issues, the chief will need to be on the front line trying to find solutions. The bureaucrats will probably only need to be reigned in occasionally.

CHAPTER 4

Stage Four:

Develop Trust With The Union

How do you develop trust? It is an easy three step process:

1. Know what you are talking about (do your homework)
2. Do what you say you will do (tell the truth)
3. Behave like a rational person

It's pretty simple, but it takes time. Not only do you have to sell yourself, you have to also overcome all transgressions committed by your predecessors. Oh yeah, those lawyers and bean counters that the city used previously who did no research and seldom knew what they were talking about. Those same guys who repeatedly told lies and thought it was a good negotiating tactic. The ones who were condescending and rude and thought the way to "victory" was through intimidation. Do not be disappointed when the union does not embrace the olive branch you are now extending. First, you must overcome all of the sins of the people before you. Okay, where do you start? Have a meeting with their leadership well before the start of negotiations. If you can, get them to go to dinner with you. Bring your spouses. Let them do most of the talking and give them a chance to ventilate. Commit yourself to always being courteous and truthful and abide by that commitment.

You will probably catch a lot of flack from the "legal eagles" for this. Blow them off. Local government contract bargaining is the only negotiating activity that I am aware of that is conducted like an IRS tax audit. That is absurd. Social interaction is a key component in virtually every major transaction in this country. It is in every state capitol. It certainly is in Washington, DC. It is the same in the private sector. Every major business transaction I have been involved with included dinner, drinks, golf, or some other social activity. It is only in local government contract negotiations that the participants look and act like grim faced bores.

However, do not try to rush this issue. You will probably have to begin negotiations with the union being very cautious and distrustful. Trust is not something that you can talk people into, either they have it or they don't. I would never discuss the word "trust" with them, it will normally backfire. I once had a foster child (6 year old boy) who liked to use the expression "that's the truth, I tell you for sure." I soon learned that he was normally lying when he used that phrase. It became almost comical. Yes, I wised him up, but today, I immediately become suspicious when I hear someone use that phrase. Asking someone to trust you is usually perceived as a warning that you are about to tell a lie.

Trust is developed from actions, not words. To earn trust, you must first prove that you are trustworthy. If you know what you are talking about, tell the truth and do not behave like a nut. Trust will slowly develop. A word of caution, although it takes time to develop trust, it can be destroyed in an instant. On several occasions when I have felt a good relationship of trust had been developed with the other negotiating team, I have seen it suddenly evaporate when the lead negotiator for the other side starts "speaking in tongues" and behaving like some late night television holy roller. I immediately raise the draw bridge and put the alligators in the moat. This is what most people will do. Unless you have a death wish, refrain from nutty talk and goofy behavior.

I cannot overemphasize the importance of not lying and not being condescending. I don't care if you have an I.Q. of 200 and the union's guy is a meathead thug, you accomplish nothing by being deceptive and insulting. Trying to present bogus and deliberately biased information is doing exactly that. It is not a bluff, it is a lie. Over my many years of working in this business, I have seen countless reports and documents that were so poorly prepared and dishonest that they did not even rise to the level of being low-grade birdcage liners. Cities and unions both do this. You can stop this on the city's side. If the union tries to do this to you, do not blow up. Ask them questions and keep asking them questions – a la Columbo. They will eventually give it up.

The "big lie" that I have seen repeatedly is the city claiming that step pay increases are causing the aggregate payroll to increase each year. It is a bogus claim. If you do not understand this, read Appendix A. It totally debunks this claim. There is one city (I will not name it) that just keeps making this claim, even after being shown repeatedly that it is just not so. They even refer to it by an acronym — SPI. Each negotiating cycle they try to make the "funding of SPI" look like a pay increase they are offering. They do it in a smug and pretentious manner. I do not know if they are really

that stupid or if they are only stupid enough to think that the union is
that stupid. Any way you slice it, this demonstrates stupidity and it
is a lie. With this single act, that city violates all three of the criteria
I have listed above.

CHAPTER 5

Stage Five:

Negotiate the Deal

Most people like things done sequentially. So, keeping with that preference here are the steps for negotiating the contract from the city's perspective:

1. Negotiate the agenda
2. State the city's goal
3. Set the impasse date
4. Identify the issues to be considered
5. Deal with the non-monetary issues
6. Depose the union
7. Estimate the union's bottom line
8. Estimate the city's top line
9. Reaffirm your authority
10. Eliminate as many issues as possible
11. Frame discussion around the union's bottom line
12. Make multiple closes

13. Draft the tentative agreement
14. Get the tentative agreement signed

Step One - Negotiate the agenda

Every negotiation has to have guidelines to operate under.
Most are benign, such as when, where, how long to meet, and
how often to meet. Don't let these small issues turn into big
disputes. When to meet should be wide open. I would try to avoid
Mondays and Fridays, as well as 8:00 A.M. on any day. Where to
meet? Sometimes this turns into a real fight. The idea of home
field advantage, such as in sports, is constantly taught at many
negotiating seminars. Personally, I think that is just baloney. People
who subscribe to this effect will want to have all negotiating
sessions at a neutral site or alternate between city hall and the
union office. I prefer to have all sessions at city hall, even when
negotiating for the union. The city usually has better and more
facilities. Also, most ad hoc information that may be needed
will be readily available at city hall. What you want to avoid is
interruptions. Cell phones should be turned off and staff given
instructions to not interrupt the meeting. If interruptions persist,
start meeting at the library or the conference room of a business in
the town.

How long to meet is something that is often misunderstood.
Marathon sessions are non-productive. Meetings of two to four
hours are adequate. Back to back meeting days are bad. There
needs to be time in between meetings – at least two weeks. There
should be informal discussions during the interim by e-mail and
telephone. Forget letters. They are too formal. This is the point
where some attorneys go wild, claiming that informal discussions
are in violation of collective bargaining laws. Stick a sock in them.

This is probably the time to set the attorney straight. He is not the captain of the ship. You are. He works in the engine room under your direction. If he does not like that, send him packing. The same applies to the other two bureaucrats. You cannot succeed with some smart mouth trying to invoke the trappings of his vocation. They can always try to get the administrator to fire you. If they can, it is better to find out right up front.

Many cities like a rigid structure that has a fixed date for various things to occur. It is good to keep the process moving, but trying to force people to do things before they are prepared may result in them doing irrational things. Let's assume that you strong arm the union into presenting all of their proposals at the first or second negotiating session. This normally results in the union asking for unreasonable items and large amounts. On the other hand, if there is some discussion of the issues without making proposals, unreasonable thoughts will usually be discarded and when they do make their proposals, they will be closer to reality. Outrageous proposals greatly increase the chances of impasse.

Having said that, I must admit most unions will try to present all of their proposals at the first session. We constantly advise them not to do this but few seem to get the point. Contract negotiations have been so commandeered by a legal process that most unions think it all begins with an indictment – their proposals. When this occurs, do not start talking about their proposals. Do not reject their proposal or start a debate. Begin asking questions about their issues and ignore the proposals. Here are some questions to ask:

1) Have you done any research concerning your pay and benefits?
2) What does that research tell you?
3) What would be some options to address those findings?
4) Over what period of time should this be addressed?
5) Are you open to brain storming for solutions?

If the premature presentation of proposals is not handled properly, negotiations will most likely end up in impasse. You certainly do not want to make the same mistake by offering a counter proposal immediately after they make theirs. There needs to be a wide open discussion before proposals are considered. Just try to stall the discussion of proposals to a later date. It is important that you do this in a non-condescending manner and do not insult them. It does not help your cause to make them mad right up front.

Another thing that most cities want is a "gag rule" – making everything confidential. Forget about that. If negotiations are at a gridlock, there may be things that need to be said publicly. This is how you communicate with the union membership and how the union communicates with the city council. I would encourage both sides to not be "spilling their guts," but there is a time and place for alternative communications. People behave differently if they know "the plug can be pulled" on them at any time. This includes you and the administrator. It is a forced discipline that all parties need.

Step Two - State The City's Goal

I am not talking about the actual agreement you want to obtain. If you state that, you will be blown up. The city's stated goal should be:

"A plan that gets pay and benefits to the proper market level."

Nothing else should be said. The unstated goal should be:

"A plan that gets pay and benefits to the proper market level without alienating our employees in the process."

This should be obvious to anyone, but it is not. Most city negotiators see the process as a highly competitive duel of will and wits with the side scoring the most points as the winner. Negotiations are conducted as if they had no affect on anything else, but they do. Whatever deal you make with your employees, whether it is minimum wage or $500,000 per year, you want to get the maximum return and benefit from their labor. You do not get that by antagonizing them. This is where I have a problem with many so-called "labor attorneys" that negotiate for cities. Negotiations are conducted as if their personal pride and ego were on the line. Their goal is to nail another raccoon pelt to the wall or add another name to their list of sexual conquests and brag to the world about their latest victory. These so called "hot shots" are not doing their employer any good. Do not behave like that.

What is the goal of negotiations in a hostage situation? I would say that it is to get the hostages free without anyone getting hurt and securing the arrest of the perpetrator. The goal of contract negotiations is the same. You should attempt to obtain the best deal for the city without creating any collateral damage. What would be collateral damage from contract negotiations? How about this:

1. A three year blizzard of grievances and lawsuits
2. Three years of pissed off employees doing the minimum amount of work
3. Three years of recalcitrant employees in the attack mode

I have been to places where the hatred created by contract negotiations is at a feverish pitch. It is horrible. I do not know how they stand it. Everyone involved, employees and management, should resign and try to start a better life somewhere else. There is no excuse for this outcome. Many times, it is the employees who instigate the hatred. It doesn't matter who gets it started. What does matter is "nipping it in the bud." That responsibility falls on you. Being part of management, you are suppose to be brighter and smarter, at least that is the rationale behind paying management more than rank and file employees. This is the time for you to employ those skills.

Step Three - Set The Impasse Date

Many employers think this idea is stupid. Their reasoning is that the longer they stall negotiations, the longer the current pay remains in place and if and when a deal is made they can avoid retro pay. It doesn't take a mathematician to figure that out. If you buy into this line of thought, go back and reread step two.

Most places should start contract negotiations about six to nine months prior to the date that next year's budget is to be approved. The impasse date should be about two months prior to that same date. If you think that prolonging negotiations helps your situation, you are mistaken. Ideally, you should try to get the deal done in about four negotiating sessions, which would be well before the proposed impasse date. If you follow public safety contract negotiations around the country, you are well aware that some of "the big boys" have marathon contract negotiations that last for years. Forget about "the big boys." They do not know what they are doing. They never reach a deal and always go to arbitration. An orangutan and a baboon could do just as well. It is in everyone's best interest to complete negotiations in a timely manner.

Next, you need to decide what will occur once impasse has been reached. You need to have a "Plan B." This concept is more important to the union than the city because the union is the one prosecuting the case. Many cities do not seem concerned about this, but they should. Unless you intend to fight with the union into the next millennium, you need to have a plan to get negotiations to some conclusion. If you have arbitration, fact-finding, or mediation then that is your "Plan B" for impasse. Once impasse is declared, get the process started. You can continue to talk with the union. Declaring impasse doesn't require that the parties throw a tantrum and storm out in a rage. In fact, it should be an unemotional event.

If you do not have a mandated impasse resolution process you will need to create a process. You can always bring in a mediator. It does not have to be a legal requirement. Another method could be changing the mix of the negotiating teams. Perhaps you may need to bring the administrator to a meeting with the union. One of the union's biggest concerns is that they are not being taken seriously. Bringing in the administrator shows that you are taking them seriously. You might get a former mayor and a retired former president of the union to attend. People who do not have a direct, current investment in negotiations can add some reason. Whatever you do, you must find a way to bring negotiations to a successful conclusion. If this is not making sense to you, go back to Step Two – State The City's Goal.

Where arbitration is available, the union is usually conditioned to going to impasse every negotiating cycle. This is because most cities do not get serious about negotiations until impasse is reached. Unfortunately, by that time the city's negotiator has already alienated the union's negotiator because he has no authority or motivation to reach a deal. Don't go down that path. There is no benefit to the city.

Step Four - Identify The Issues To Be Discussed

Issues to be discussed are topics, not amounts or proposals. One issue is always there – the base pay matrix. Actually, there are only two issues:

1. More money
2. More restrictions on the chief

Everything else is just the details as to the way that these changes will manifest themselves. Any changes that cost money are more money. Some of these are:

1. Base Pay
2. Longevity
3. Shift Pay
4. Education Pay
5. Health Insurance
6. Retiree Insurance
7. Pension Contribution
8. Vacation
9. Holidays
10. Sick Leave
11. Personal Leave

All of these items should be negotiated between you and the union's negotiating team. Your focus needs to be on the total compensation, not individual components. A city that may be willing to raise base pay by 3 percent will probably only agree to a lower amount if other items of compensation are increased. One of the objectives of identifying the issues is to eliminate those that will not be discussed. The purpose of this is not to box the union into a corner, but to try to restrict the discussion to the real issues. Otherwise, there can never be a global evaluation of the total impact if new issues continue to pop up.

Step Five – Deal With The Non-Monetary Issues

Non-monetary issues fall into the "more restrictions on the chief" category and need to be handled differently. To advance or dispose of these issues there need to be negotiations between the chief and the union — away from the table. The negotiating table is not the proper venue for non-monetary issues. The easiest thing for you to do is just tell the chief and the union negotiators to work it out. Unfortunately, that will probably not succeed. Ideally, the chief and union will have already dealt with the issues as they arose and they are only bringing them up to codify them in the contract. The fact that they are being raised as issues at the negotiating table tells you that this has not occurred.

Okay, so what should you do? I would set up a meeting between the chief and the union's lead negotiator with you serving as a mediator. Do this in the chief's office. He will feel less threatened in his office. Exclude everyone, except the three of you, especially the attorneys. Many times, the union has a long list of these operational issues, which typically focus on discipline, promotions, grievances, and duty assignments. Most of the issues will be spurious and will have little merit or rationale. Your first task is to prune the list down to a workable number. You do this by asking the union guy questions:

1) Why is this issue a problem?
2) How often does it come into play?
3) How important is it to you?
4) What is your solution?
5) How do you think the chief will react?

Next, you seek the chief's thoughts, by asking questions:

1. How can we make this issue go away?
2. What are your thoughts about the union's solution?
3. What new problems would this create?
4. What is your solution?
5. How do you think the union will react?

The real struggle is getting these two guys to behave. The union will invariably give goofy rationale for many of their issues. The issue may have never occurred, but they think it might in the future. The only reason they can give for wanting this change is just that they want it. The real reason they want the changes is because they do not trust the chief. The chief does not trust them either. That's a shame, but there is not much you can do to overcome the distrust. You may be able to mitigate it a little. The chief will try to avoid the issues and make non-specific objections such as "I'm the chief" and "I just don't like it" or "it will weaken my power." It is very similar to you refusing something to your teenage son. How far does "because I say so" or "I'm your father" get you? Well, it doesn't work here either. Most of the items that the union wants are goofy or even worse. If they were not, they would most likely already be in place. Most union contracts already have too many restrictions on the chief. Still, the new issues have to be dealt with and eliminated using common sense and rationale. They cannot be ignored. This is what the chief would prefer to do.

So how do you get these two hardheads to play ball? The union guy is your responsibility. There is no one else to do it. Get him off to the side and tell him that he can either be obstinate and get nothing or cooperate and get some of the issues that are legitimate. Be sure that he understands that the administrator is not going to cram these things down the chief's throat and that an arbitrator probably will not either. It's simple. Drop the nonsense and talk about real issues.

The chief presents a different problem. You can try reasoning with him, but if he is already in the "stupid speak" mode you most likely will not accomplish anything. This is where you will need the administrator to put the heat on him. You might even need to have the chief attend a meeting in the administrator's office. The chief will not like this. This may sound rather extreme, but sometimes people can really be hardheaded. What you want to do is eliminate all or most of the issues. You cannot do that without the chief participating. Unless you dispose of these issues, they are going to linger around forever.

Step Six – Depose The Union

Now that the non-monetary issues have been sent to a venue away from the table, it is time to address the monetary issues. You begin by deposing the union. You want to get the answer to that famous question – what did he know and when did he know it? You learn the answer by asking a whole lot of questions. Your mission with this step is to find out all of the union's thoughts and rationale for each monetary issue being raised. Get copies of all of their research and accompanying reports. When you get through with this step, you want to know:

1) What they want
2) Why they want it
3) Why they think they should get it
4) What evidence do they have to support it

It is very important that you not try to attack their thoughts or supporting evidence. You also do not want to begin a debate. Now is not the time to question their motivations or research. You only want to ask those questions after you have collected all of the information you can and have had time to analyze it. This is not a skeet shoot. You do not have to shoot down everything as it comes out of the box. Heck, you do not have to shoot down anything at any time if you play it correctly. Stupid ideas eventually fade away. The sponsor's brain will finally kick in.

Step Seven – Estimate The Union's Bottom Line

The bottom line is the least amount that the union will agree to. That is not necessarily the "bottom line" that they are telling you. Surprise, they understand the use of mendacity also. It takes some detective work to estimate the real number. The following data should help you determine this number:

1) The current rate of inflation
2) Raises being received by other departments
3) How your department compares with other departments

Let's assume that the current rate of inflation is 2.5 percent and most other departments in the area are getting about 3 percent raises and your department is currently 6 percent behind the market. Most unions would probably walk before accepting anything less than 3 percent. Otherwise they would fall further behind their peer departments. My guess is that their bottom line is 3.5 percent.

They will be asking for much more, but given a big enough dose of reality would settle for their bottom line. But, they are most likely thinking that some improvement will have to be made in relation to the market or their membership will be all over the leadership.

Step Eight – Estimate The City's Top Bottom Line

The top line is the most that the city will agree to. Let's assume that we are negotiating a three year contract and our goal is to get our department to market average. However, we do not think it is politically feasible to get there in only three years. We feel like we can cut it in half during the term of the new contract without getting a political firestorm started. Based on this, we would want to match the 3 percent that other departments are getting plus an additional 1 percent each year. This makes our target number 4 percent, which is above the union's estimated bottom line. However, we need to set the maximum we would go to reach an agreement, knowing that it will take six years to close the market gap with 4 percent annual raises. If we are a little high for the first contract (years 1 through 3), we possibly can make it up on the second contract (years 4 through 6). One thing we can be relatively certain about is that wages will go up, not down. This gives us some room for correction if we overdo it now. So, we decide that our top line is 4.5 percent, but we want to reach agreement at 4 percent.

Based on the estimates for the union's bottom line and the city's top line, we now have the "strike zone" established. Any agreement will have to between 3.5 percent and 4.5 percent, which leaves our goal in the middle. Hopefully, the union has not made any proposals yet, or they have, but have long since relegated them to the ash can. Now would be a good time for them to submit a proposal. If it is within the realm of reason (5 percent or less) then you should submit a counter. If their initial proposal is 5 percent, you should counter with 3 percent, which is within your range of authority – 4 percent. Obviously, to reach an agreement you both will have to be pitching the same percentage. That means that one or both of you will have to modify your position. Everyone knows that seldom is an opening proposal the final amount. Both sides know that there will be movement on each side. At some point it is customary for the union to make a counter proposal – 4.5 percent. Preempt that move by making a counter proposal of 3.5 percent (their bottom line) and immediately begin a dialogue using the 3.5 percent as an anchor. It is a lot easier for you to sell their bottom line than it is for you to reject your top line – 4.5 percent. Your goal should continue to be 4 percent. They will have a different goal – your top line of 4.5 percent. You want to try to get to the optimal amount – 4 percent, but the union wants to get as much as possible. If it appeared that an agreement is being reached at an amount below 4 percent, you would probably want to relax your resistance and allow the amount to creep up. The union would never do that. You want to come in on the mark. The union is only concerned with not coming in under the mark. Remember, you want to strike a deal at the best price for the city's overall interest. This is not a limbo contest where you try to go as low as you can.

Step Nine – Reaffirm Your Authority

As soon as it appears that a settlement is possible you need to reaffirm your authority with the administrator. You want to be absolutely certain that any tentative agreement you sign is not repudiated, so you do not want to be in the position of having to seek that approval once you have reached agreement. Have that authority before reaching agreement.

Step Ten – Eliminate as Many Issues as Possible

The ideal tentative agreement should have few items of change. It is better to have a big change to the pay matrix than it is to have a laundry list of small changes that come to the same cost. Keep the base pay matrix as the last item. This prevents nibbling once an agreement is obtained. Nibbling is asking for $50 more clothing allowance or an extra holiday. Once you get to the final number on the pay matrix all of the other possible issues should have been dispatched. I have seen nibbling destroy the entire deal. Kill it before it kills the deal.

Step Eleven – Frame the Discussion Around the Union's Bottom Line

As we get close to a deal, we want to focus entirely on the union's bottom line. It doesn't matter if the amount being discussed is higher. Just keep the ball on their end of the field – below your goal number – 4 percent. The more reasonable you make their bottom line sound, the sweeter the deal you are offering looks. No matter what the final outcome is, the union has to feel that it accomplished something and they will if you conduct negotiations properly. They have done better than their bottom line. They didn't get you to your top line, which was their real goal, but they got something that will improve their position in the market.

Step Twelve – Make Multiple Closes

I teach unions to never attempt to close, but you must make the closing move. If you have done your job properly you will be comfortable with the results of negotiations, but the union may be hesitant. They are afraid they may be leaving money on the table. It is similar to you buying a new car. You are afraid that you might over pay. As a result, you need some encouragement to sign the deal. The same thoughts are going through the union negotiator's head. At this point, you need to help relieve the union's anxiety and apprehension. They are already sold; they just still have some doubts.

Step Thirteen – Write the Tentative Agreement

Who should write the tentative agreement? You and the union's lead negotiator should write it together. Do not let the attorneys do it. And under no circumstances should you let the two attorneys speak to each other. Most of these guys do not know how to make deals. They only know how to screw things up. Write everything in the vernacular. Skip all of that legal crap. It is nothing but pompous baloney that leads to disputes. Use short, single clause, declarative sentences that include few participles and commas, and never use semicolons. If you leave a pinhole of doubt, some overzealous lawyer will be suing. Contracts are meant to be understood. They are not literary works of art. It is okay to have your attorney look over the agreement, but only in the capacity of an advisor. I cannot emphasize this enough. When an attorney says "let me get some of these details cleaned up" he is really saying "let me stab your deal in the heart." Get over being intimidated by attorneys and take charge of the process.

Step Fourteen – Get The Tentative Agreement Signed

Who should sign the tentative agreement? Everyone on both negotiating teams should sign the agreement. There should be a signature block for each person. You want 100 percent buy in. If someone refuses to sign, it is best to know now. You can then thwart their "Trojan Horse" play. This is where someone who is part of the negotiating team works against ratification. The person most likely to do this is the city's attorney. On the night of ratification at the city council meeting, he is up there pretending to be King Solomon and giving your agreement the coup de grace. You have to take that sucker out in advance. As soon as you identify someone on your team as a Trojan, expose him and go straight to the administrator to get him to put the muscle on the defector. If it is someone on the union's team, speak with the union's lead negotiator in private and be certain that he has an effective plan for dealing with his maverick. This is the time to forget about being nice and to attack the Trojan. You have to mortally wound his ploy.

CHAPTER 6

Stage Six:

Get the Deal Ratified

Most people think that ratification is just a formality that is automatic. It is not. If this step is not handled correctly, everything you have accomplished can go up in smoke. Two groups will have to approve the agreement — the city council and the union members. Every argument given as a reason for ratifying to one group can be an argument for the other group to not ratify. Unless the votes are taken at the same time, one group will already know the outcome of the vote by the other group and the arguments presented to that group. Overselling it at the first vote may cause a defeat at the second vote. If the union's president gives an over-the-top presentation to the city council claiming that the tentative agreement is really a good deal for the city, he may have it voted down by his membership the following night.

So, how do you get the deal ratified? First, I would let the union vote on it. They are the most volatile. Besides, if you have done your job properly, you already know the vote for the council. Otherwise, you would not have agreed to the tentative agreement. The union has more of a mob mentality. First of all, there are many more of them than there are city councilors. The city will have the press and everybody else watching them. The union vote will be conducted in a closed meeting, far from the press and the public. It is much easier to get a revolt started there. Once the union approves it, the council can vote in a controlled environment.

What should be said to the union membership and the city council? Something like this:

> *"This is a fair deal for both the city and the employees. It is less than what the employees would like to have, but it is more than what the city initially offered. Both sides can live with this deal. It is in the best interest of all parties, employees and citizens, that this agreement be ratified."*

Some Closing Thoughts

Who Should be On the City's Negotiating Team?

One thing to keep in mind is that the smaller the negotiating teams, the better the chances are for coming to an agreement. The larger the negotiating teams, the more posturing occurs. Ideally, there is only one person on each team. Rarely does this happen because both the city and union are scared of this arrangement. I do not understand that thinking. Maybe they think that the other side's negotiator will hypnotize their negotiator or maybe they fear collusion. Whatever it is, few places are buying it. If I were the lead negotiator for the city, I would only want one other person on the team, probably the human resources director, or maybe an assistant administrator. I certainly would not want the twin grim reapers – the city attorney and the finance director. However, there are times that they may be forced on you. Sometimes they are really good people to have on your team. I've known some attorneys and finance directors I would like to have on my team, but I cannot remember very many. I'm a "bean counter" myself. Sometimes I can hardly stand me.

Should the Chief Attend Negotiations?

Yes, he should. He should not be on either side of the table. He should be sitting at the end or head of the table. He should be there to represent the department. Let me assure you, the interest of the department is not always congruent with the city and union interests. Let's assume that one of the items being negotiated is eliminating shift pay and putting it into the pay matrix. The union wants it and the city does not care how the money is allocated. The chief, on the other hand, has a serious problem with this proposal. Shifts and days off are bid by seniority. If there are no monetary shift incentives all the senior guys will be working the day shift and all the new guys will be working midnights. The chief explains that for this to work, shift bidding would have to be replaced with mandatory rotations. That's okay with the city, but the union wants no part of that plan. The proper outcome is probably to leave things as they are.

What Kind of Records Should There Be of the Negotiating Sessions?

None!! This is another idea where the lawyers go crazy. I have a habit of causing that. I have been to negotiating sessions that had no record keeping, except for a few personal notes by the participants. I have also seen detailed handwritten notes taken by both sides. I have been to sessions with tape recorders employed. And the over-the-top award goes to the cities where they actually had a court reporter taking down verbatim testimony, complete with real time transcripts. Wow, isn't technology great? Yeah, it is, but in this case it sucks. Detailed note keeping, tape recorders, and stenographers are the death knell for negotiations. Who cares what someone said. What matters is what he is willing to admit he said. I once was involved with contract negotiations that had a stenographer. The first session we all maintained a formal posture and asked carefully crafted questions, which were answered with equally carefully crafted answers. Not much was accomplished at that meeting, other than agreeing to have lunch at 12:00. At the second session, everyone was armed with transcripts from the first session and a process of parsing every word began, followed by a debate over semantics that lasted all day. The third session was just like the first, and the fourth was just like the second. Luckily, there was a collective bargaining law there which required that negotiations be completed within a couple of months or the issues are submitted to arbitration. Ditch the tape recorder and the stenographer.

What Should My Demeanor Be? Tough as Nails or Conciliatory?

Neither, you need to be the voice of reason. Being tough bombs, unless your goal is to piss off the other side and get nothing accomplished. Being conciliatory usually results in the other side being too aggressive and talks stall because they have staked out too high of a position. Just be yourself and deal with the union team just as you would with anyone else. Do not let things get blown out of proportion. If the average guy in the department is making $60,000 and we think the strike zone for settlement is somewhere between 3.5 percent and 4.5 percent, we are only talking about a difference of $600. That's hardly anything to get hysterical about. If the union gets your top line, the pay next year will be $62,700. If you get the union to their bottom line, it will be $62,100. Regardless of the outcome, no employee is going to have his house foreclosed and the city is not going broke. You are not negotiating to determine if pay will be minimum wage or $150,000. It is all about $600.

What if the Union Tries to Play Tough?

Let them. You can only control your behavior. Do the correct things that we have discussed. Do not be focused on controlling the outcome. Only control the things you can control – your thoughts and actions. Never engage in arguments or debates. At some point you may have to tell them what the options are – either try to reach an agreement or go to "Plan B." Do not be hesitant to declare impasse, especially if the union is being abusive. I give the same advice to them. If we are not getting anywhere, why beat our heads against the wall. Not reaching an agreement is not a reflection on you if you have done the right things. You have to have the courage to pull the trigger.

What if the Union Negotiator is Wimpy?

I know, you are thinking "what a deal." However, the weak opponent provides two problems. First, it may be virtually impossible to get a decision out of him, because he is probably full of doubt. Second, he may never be able to get a negotiated deal ratified by his members. Actually, I hate this situation. You will need to immediately begin a program of rehabilitation to instill some confidence in him. This may require you negotiating both sides. You need to get him to a point of self-confidence that he can make a final decision. Next, he has to leave the negotiations with the appearance of accomplishing something. If you just slam dunk him, you will never get a deal. Remember, your goal is to get an agreement, even if this means propping the other guy up on the dance floor until the song is over. If it looks like he got his butt whipped, your deal is probably toast.

Isn't There Some Way Other Than Negotiations?

Oh sure, except that it does not work. You could do all of the research and determine the "exact price" for wages and then present it on day one. I wouldn't. It will only get you to impasse. People need to feel that they make an impact by applying their persuasion skills. Otherwise, that old hippy philosophy of "the futility of endeavor" is correct. Hopefully, you do not subscribe to it. You could give them the "take it or leave it" ultimatum. If their Plan B is weaker than yours then you may be able to impose your will, but look out. They will get their revenge, either monetarily or by inflicting pain. If you do not believe this, try that approach on your wife or husband. Good luck! About the only way to avoid negotiating is to hire someone to do it for you. No matter how it is handled, you will eventually become involved.

Several years ago, car dealers went to a "no haggle" pricing system – the price on the windshield was the actual selling price. The theory was that this would relieve buyer's anxiety and make selling easier. Even purchasers thought it would be an improvement. However, that did not last long. Regardless of any factual basis, buyers began to suspect that there was still some price inflation in the "no haggle" price. This left buyers feeling uncertain and led to an increase in buyer's remorse. You cannot avoid negotiating. Negotiations are to deals what foreplay is to sex.

Appendix A

The Step Plan Cost Myth

One of the most common myths about a step pay plan is that there is a constant annual increase in total payroll costs as the result of the step increases. The following illustrations show the fallacy of this claim. All pay increases are offset by the savings from people leaving at higher steps and being replaced by new people at the beginning step. Freezing a step pay plan causes the payroll to decline. No pay increases are given, but there continues to be savings from people leaving. Eventually, all employees are at the starting level. There are certain facts that are obvious.

The first of these facts is that every employee that receives a step increases causes an increase in payroll cost. The second fact is that every employee that does not get a step increase has no impact on payroll cost. The final fact is that every employee that leaves, except a first year hire, causes payroll cost to decline.

In case you are hung up on the last fact, consider that when someone leaves the department by any manner – quits, fired, death, disability, or retirement – who replaces him? Assume that there are 300 people in the department and one quits. This leaves 299 employees. Who takes the empty place on the payroll? Is it a person that is paid the same or more than the one leaving? (If you cannot figure this out, just toss this book and continue with your ignorance.) Obviously, it is a new hire making starting pay.

Look at Exhibit A on the next page. It shows a department with 30 employees that are all one year apart. Eighteen employees get a step increase, eleven get none, and one goes "wee, wee, wee" all the way home and is replaced by a new man. There would never be an exact and equal distribution, but the effect is unchanged.

Look at the following exhibits closely. How do you get to step 5? By first going through steps 1 through 4. How do you get to step 30? By going through steps 1 through 29. When you exit, where does the new man come in? Step 1. If you are still not convinced, get out your Excel worksheet and try it for yourself. I tell you what I would do. I would forget about proving the step pay increase myth and find a new hobby. Once you have given up on this idea, you can tackle the real topics that will affect negotiations.

As shown in Exhibit B, an employee does not have to be at step 30 to generate savings. Anyone leaving after the first year creates savings. Don't start making excuses for things like promotion. Use your brain. If you still cannot figure all of this out, give us an anonymous telephone call and we will try to help you. Once you see the light, you will be glad you did not reveal your identity. Don't trust me. I may be tempted to tell names.

Exhibit A - Cost of Step Pay Increases			
Year	**Pay 2007**	**Pay 2008**	**Increase**
Hired		$38,875	$38,875	New Hire For 2008
1	$38,875	$39,874	$999	
2	$39,874	$40,851	$977	
3	$40,851	$41,766	$915	
4	$41,766	$42,869	$1,103	
5	$42,869	$43,930	$1,061	
6	$43,930	$44,970	$1,040	
7	$44,970	$53,352	$8,382	
8	$53,352	$54,746	$1,394	
9	$54,746	$56,035	$1,289	
10	$56,035	$57,450	$1,415	
11	$57,450	$58,906	$1,456	
12	$58,906	$60,320	$1,414	
13	$60,320	$61,828	$1,508	
14	$61,828	$63,374	$1,546	
15	$63,374	$64,958	$1,584	
16	$64,958	$66,582	$1,624	
17	$66,582	$68,247	$1,665	
18	$68,247	$69,953	$1,706	
19	$69,953	$69,953	$0	
20	$69,953	$69,953	$0	
21	$69,953	$69,953	$0	
22	$69,953	$69,953	$0	
23	$69,953	$69,953	$0	
24	$69,953	$69,953	$0	
25	$69,953	$69,953	$0	
26	$69,953	$69,953	$0	
27	$69,953	$69,953	$0	
28	$69,953	$69,953	$0	
29	$69,953	$69,953	$0	
30	$69,953	$0	-$69,953	Employee Retires
Totals	**$1,798,369**	**$1,798,369**	**$0**	

Exhibit B - Savings from Terminations		
Year		
1	$38,875	$0
2	$39,874	$999
3	$40,851	$1,976
4	$41,766	$2,891
5	$42,869	$3,994
6	$43,930	$5,055
7	$44,970	$6,095
8	$53,352	$14,477
9	$54,746	$15,871
10	$56,035	$17,160
11	$57,450	$18,575
12	$58,906	$20,031
13	$60,320	$21,445
14	$61,828	$22,953
15	$63,374	$24,499
16	$64,958	$26,083
17	$66,582	$27,707
18	$68,247	$29,372
19	$69,953	$31,078
20	$69,953	$31,078
21	$69,953	$31,078
22	$69,953	$31,078
23	$69,953	$31,078
24	$69,953	$31,078
25	$69,953	$31,078
26	$69,953	$31,078
27	$69,953	$31,078
28	$69,953	$31,078
29	$69,953	$31,078
30	$69,953	$31,078

Appendix B

Past and Current Client Listing

ARKANSAS
Jacksonville Fraternal Order of Police

CALIFORNIA
Arcadia Police Officers' Association
Del Norte County Sheriff Employees Association
Fresno County Deputy Sheriffs Association
Fullerton Police Officers' Association
Hanford Police Officers' Association
Long Beach Police Officers' Association
Ontario Police Officers' Association and the City of Ontario
Pomona Police Officers' Association and the City of Pomona
Whittier Police Officers' Association

COLORADO

Adams County Fraternal Order of Police

Arvada (Colorado Fraternal Order of Police)

Denver Police Protective Association

Denver Fraternal Order of Police (Sheriff Deputies)

Englewood Police Benefit Association

Ft. Collins (Northern Colorado Fraternal Order of Police)

Lakewood (Colorado Fraternal Order of Police)

Larimer County Fraternal Order of Police

Las Animas County (Colorado Fraternal Order of Police)

CONNECTICUT

Newington International Brotherhood of Police Officers' Local 443

Stamford Police Association

DISTRICT OF COLUMBIA

United States Capitol Police Labor Committee

FLORIDA

Boca Raton Fraternal Order of Police

Tallahassee (Big Bend Police Benevolent Association)

Volusia County (International Brotherhood of Teamsters, Local 385)

ILLINOIS

Chicago Fraternal Order of Police

DeKalb County Metropolitan Alliance of Police, Chapter 318

Rock Island (International Association of Fire Fighters, Local 26)

Sycamore Fraternal Order of Police

INDIANA

Indianapolis Fraternal Order of Police

KANSAS

Dodge City Fraternal Order of Police

Edwardsville Fraternal Order of Police

Hays Fraternal Order of Police

Hutchinson Fraternal Order of Police

Hutchinson (International Association of Fire Fighters)

Manhattan (Riley County Fraternal Order of Police)

Kansas City Fraternal Order of Police

Kansas Troopers' Association (state troopers)

Lawrence Fraternal Order of Police

Leavenworth Fraternal Order of Police

Olathe Fraternal Order of Police

Sedgwick County (International Association of Fire Fighters)

Topeka Fraternal Order of Police

Topeka (International Association of Fire Fighters)

Wichita Fraternal Order of Police

Wichita (International Association of Fire Fighters)

Wyandotte County Fraternal Order of Police

KENTUCKY

Lexington (Bluegrass Fraternal Order of Police)

Louisville (River City Fraternal Order of Police)

Paducah (Jackson Purchase Fraternal Order of Police)

LOUISIANA

Alexandria Police Officers' Association

Baton Rouge Union of Police

Hammond Union of Police

Lake Charles Police Officers' Association

New Iberia Policeman's Association

MASSACHUSETTS

Boston Police Patrolmen's Association

Canton Police Association

Charlton Police Alliance

Dover Police Association

Franklin Police Association

Ipswich Police Officers' Association

New Bedford Police Union

North Attleboro Police Officers' Association

North Attleboro Professional Police Officers' Association

Rockport Police Association

Saugus Police Patrol Officers' Union

Sharon Police Association

Westford Police Association

Wrentham Police Association

MICHIGAN

Kalamazoo Public Safety Officer's Association

Kalamazoo County Sheriff's Deputies Association

MINNESOTA

St. Paul Police Federation

MISSOURI

Grandview Fraternal Order of Police

Hannibal Fraternal Order of Police

Independence Fraternal Order of Police

Jackson County Fraternal Order of Police

Kansas City Police Officers' Association

Lebanon (Greater Ozark's Police Officer's Association

Lee's Summit Fraternal Order of Police

Liberty Fraternal Order of Police

Pettis County Fraternal Order of Police
Raytown Fraternal Order of Police
Sedalia Fraternal Order of Police
Springfield Police Officers' Association
St. Charles Fraternal Order of Police
St. Joseph Fraternal Order of Police
St. Louis Fraternal Order of Police
St. Louis County Fraternal Order of Police

MONTANA
Missoula Police Association

NEBRASKA
Grand Island Fraternal Order of Police
Omaha Police Union

NEVADA
Boulder City Police Protective Association
Clark County Schools Police Officers' Association
Las Vegas Police Protective Association
North Las Vegas Police Officers' Association
Nye County Sheriff's Deputy Officers' Association

NEW JERSEY
Freehold Borough PBA #159

NEW MEXICO
Albuquerque Police Officers' Association

NEW YORK
Buffalo Police Benevolent Association

Nassau County Detectives Association
New York State Correctional Officers' and Police Benevolent
Association, Inc.

OHIO
Beachwood Fraternal Order of Police
Cleveland Police Patrolmen Association
Cleveland Fraternal Order of Police
Fostoria (Ohio Patrolmen's Benevolent Association)
Ohio State Trooper's Association
Springfield Police Patrolmen's Association
Youngstown Police Association

OKLAHOMA
Ada Fraternal Order of Police
Altus Fraternal Order of Police
Bartlesville Fraternal Order of Police
Bethany Fraternal Order of Police
Bixby Fraternal Order of Police
Broken Arrow Fraternal Order of Police
Broken Arrow (International Association of Fire Fighters)
Calera Fraternal Order of Police
Catoosa Fraternal Order of Police
Chickasha Fraternal Order of Police
Choctaw Fraternal Order of Police
Claremore Fraternal Order of Police
Clinton Fraternal Order of Police
Coweta Fraternal Order of Police
Del City Fraternal Order of Police
Duncan Fraternal Order of Police
Durant Fraternal Order of Police
Durant (International Association of Fire Fighters)

Edmond Fraternal Order of Police

El Reno Fraternal Order of Police

Enid Fraternal Order of Police

Guthrie Fraternal Order of Police

Hugo Fraternal Order of Police

Jenks Fraternal Order of Police

McAlester Fraternal Order of Police

Miami Fraternal Order of Police

Midwest City Fraternal Order of Police

Moore Fraternal Order of Police

Muskogee Fraternal Order of Police

Mustang Fraternal Order of Police

Nichols Hills Fraternal Order of Police

Noble Fraternal Order of Police

Norman Fraternal Order of Police

Norman (International Association of Fire Fighters)

Oklahoma City Fire Fighters Association

Okmulgee Fraternal Order of Police

Okmulgee (International Association of Fire Fighters)

Owasso Fraternal Order of Police

Perry Fraternal Order of Police

Ponca City Fraternal Order of Police

Sallisaw Fraternal Order of Police

Sand Springs Fraternal Order of Police

Sapulpa Fraternal Order of Police

Seminole Fraternal Order of Police

Skiatook Fraternal Order of Police

Stillwater Fraternal Order of Police

Tulsa Fraternal Order of Police

OREGON

Port of Portland Police AFSCME Local 1847

PENNSYLVANIA

Bristol Township Police Benevolent Association

Police Association of Falls Township

Middletown Police Benevolent Association

SOUTH DAKOTA

Minnehaha County Fraternal Order of Police

Rapid City Fraternal Order of Police

Sioux Falls Fraternal Order of Police

TENNESSEE

Franklin Fraternal Order of Police

Nashville Fraternal Order of Police

TEXAS

Abilene Police Officers' Association

Austin Police Association

Bexar County Deputy Sheriffs Association

Corpus Christi Police Officers' Association

Dallas Police Association

Denton County Fraternal Order of Police

Department of Public Safety Officers' Association

Jefferson County Association Of Deputy Sheriff's And Correction Officers'

Killeen Fraternal Order of Police

Midland Fraternal Order of Police

Montgomery County Law Enforcement Association

Odessa Fraternal Order of Police

Port Arthur Police Officers' Association

Round Rock Police Protective Association and The City Of Round Rock

San Angelo Fraternal Order of Police

UTAH
Salt Lake County Deputy Sheriffs Federation

VIRGINIA
Fairfax County Coalition of Police, Local 5000

WASHINGTON
Kennewick Police Officer's Benefit Association

Vancouver Police Officer's Guild

WEST VIRGINIA
Fairmont Fraternal Order of Police

Princeton Fraternal Order of Police

Wheeling Fraternal Order of Police

ABOUT POLICEPAY

What is POLICEPAY.NET?

POLICEPAY.NET is a consulting firm that has been assisting in public safety contract negotiations for more than twenty years. We are not a labor union or a municipal league. We do not replace these organizations or compete with them. We only concentrate on one narrow niche – contract negotiations. By restricting ourselves to this single activity, we have been able to become market leaders for new and innovative approaches to contract negotiations.

How can POLICEPAY.NET help us?

POLICEPAY.NET can see to it that contract negotiations are conducted in an intelligent and rational manner that will greatly increase your chances of obtaining an agreement that is equitable for both the employees and the employer. Our goal is to get you to that agreement without destroying the relationship between the employer and the employees. We take emotions out of the process and replace them with reasoning.

What does POLICEPAY.NET do?

POLICEPAY.NET provides three different levels of service. First, we provide state of the art research that covers market prices, costing, and finances. We show you how well you are competing with the market and what it would take to improve your market position.

Secondly, we teach and assist you in your relationship with the other side, the public, and the decision makers in your community. A good relationship with your counterparts is imperative. We teach you how to deal with the expectations of your constituents. Success is ultimately determined by whether you met their expectations.

The third level of service is serving as your negotiator throughout the entire process.

ABOUT POLICEPAY

What does POLICEPAY.NET cost?

POLICEPAY.NET has a unique pricing structure – a fixed, predetermined, turnkey price that includes travel and other related expenses. We sign a contract that shows the total cost for everything. There are no hourly rates or surprise costs. We will be glad to provide you a bid.

How do we pay POLICEPAY.NET?

POLICEPAY.NET provides several payment options, ranging from all up front to payments over 24 months. If there is a way for you to use our services, we will find it.

What is POLICEPAY.NET's methodology?

POLICEPAY.NET uses a collaborative methodology. That does not mean that we fall on our sword to make a deal, but we do not deliberately engage in hostilities and conflict. We would if those things worked – they don't.

Who can hire POLICEPAY.NET?

POLICEPAY.NET will work only for you or we will work for both sides. This is what makes POLICEPAY.NET different from others. If both sides hire us, neither of you have to deal with the other. We meet with the employees in the morning and with the employer in the afternoon. It is all done at your place of business. But hang onto your hat. This will not be an old time revival meeting that praises your side and castigates the other side. It will look and feel like a mandatory settlement conference. To each side it will look like we are working for the other side. We aren't, but to obtain an agreement, it will require that both sides move into the zone of possible agreement. Our job is to get both parties there, kicking and screaming if necessary. One thing that we require is honesty and integrity. We do not see deception as a valid negotiating tactic.

www.ingramcontent.com/pod-product-compliance
Lightning Source LLC
Chambersburg PA
CBHW030029290326
41934CB00005B/547